"University of Flavor: The Sweet Heat Grilling Handbook"

"Your Guide to Flavor Perfection"

Troy washington

Contents

Introduction 4

Beef Recipes 5

Spicy Sweet Heat Beef Skewers................................ 6
Sweet Heat Grilled Ribeye Steaks............................. 7
Sweet Heat BBQ Beef Brisket 8
Grilled Sweet Heat Burgers 9
Sweet Heat Glazed Meatballs 10
Sweet Heat Beef Short Ribs 11
Sweet Heat Steak Tacos 12
Sweet Heat Beef Stir-Fry 13
Sweet Heat Stuffed Bell Peppers 14
Sweet Heat Chili 15

Pork Recipes 16

Sweet Heat Grilled Pork Chops 17
Sweet Heat Pulled Pork Sliders.............................. 18
Sweet Heat Glazed Pork Ribs 19
Sweet Heat Pork Tenderloin 20
Sweet Heat Pork Belly Burnt Ends 21
Sweet Heat Pork Skewers..................................... 22
Sweet Heat Stuffed Pork Loin 23
Sweet Heat Pork Sausage Patties............................. 24
Sweet Heat Pork Fried Rice.................................. 25
Sweet Heat BBQ Pork Meatballs............................... 26

Seafood Recipes 27

Sweet Heat Grilled Salmon 28
Sweet Heat Shrimp Skewers 29
Sweet Heat Glazed Tilapia................................... 30
Sweet Heat Crab Cakes 31

Sweet Heat Lobster Tails 32
Sweet Heat Scallops 33
Sweet Heat Shrimp Tacos 34
Sweet Heat Grilled Mahi-Mahi. 35
Sweet Heat Seafood Paella 36
Sweet Heat Baked Cod. 37

Grilled Chicken Recipes **38**
Sweet Heat Grilled Chicken Thighs 39
Honey Lime Glazed Chicken Breasts. 40
Spicy Grilled Buffalo Drumsticks. 41
Mango-Chipotle Chicken Wings 42
Lemon Herb Spatchcock Chicken 43
Sweet Heat Chicken Skewers 44
BBQ Bacon-Wrapped Chicken Tenders 45
Coconut Curry Grilled Chicken Thighs 46
Sweet Heat BBQ Pulled Chicken Sandwiches 47
Peach Bourbon Glazed Chicken Halves 48

Vegetable Recipes. **49**
Sweet Heat Grilled Vegetable Medley 50
Sweet Heat Roasted Brussels Sprouts. 51
Sweet Heat Glazed Carrots 52
Sweet Heat Stuffed Bell Peppers 53
Sweet Heat Spiced Cauliflower Steaks 54
Sweet Heat Roasted Sweet Potatoes 55
Sweet Heat Grilled Portobello Mushrooms 56
Sweet Heat SautÃ©ed Green Beans. 57
Sweet Heat Baked Zucchini Fries. 58
Sweet Heat BBQ Veggie Skewers 59
About the Author: 60

Introduction

Welcome to University of Flavor, where every dish becomes a masterpiece and every cook is a student of bold, unforgettable tastes. Founded with the belief that great food starts with great flavor, University of Flavor is more than just a brand—it's a journey of culinary discovery.

At its core, University of Flavor combines passion, quality, and innovation to create products that elevate everyday cooking into extraordinary experiences. Whether you're a grill master, a home chef, or just someone who loves experimenting in the kitchen, our signature creations, Sweet Heat Sauce and All-Purpose Seasoning, are crafted to bring out the best in every bite.

- Sweet Heat Sauce delivers the perfect balance of sweetness and spice, transforming simple meals into showstopping dishes.
- All-Purpose Seasoning adds depth and dimension to everything it touches, from meats to vegetables and beyond.

At University of Flavor, we believe in taking your culinary skills to the next level—one recipe at a time. Let's turn your kitchen into a classroom for creativity, where you'll explore bold flavors, uncover new techniques, and craft meals that bring people together.

University of Flavor: Your taste buds' ultimate education.

Beef Recipes

University of Flavor: The Sweet Heat Grilling Handbook

Spicy Sweet Heat Beef Skewers

15 mins (+30 mins marinating)

Ingredients

- Beef sirloin (cubed, 1 lb)
- University of Flavor Sweet Heat Sauce (1/4 cup)
- All-Purpose Seasoning (2 tbsp)
- Red onion
- Bell peppers

Steps

1. Marinate beef cubes in Sweet Heat Sauce and All-Purpose Seasoning.
2. Skewer with onion and peppers, and grill for 4-5 mins per side.

University of Flavor: The Sweet Heat Grilling Handbook

Sweet Heat Grilled Ribeye Steaks

Cooking Time: 20 mins

Ingredients

- Ribeye steaks (2)
- University of Flavor Sweet Heat Sauce (1/4 cup)
- All-Purpose Seasoning (2 tbsp)
- olive oil (2 tbsp)

Steps

1. Rub steaks with olive oil and All-Purpose Seasoning.
2. Grill to desired doneness, brushing with Sweet Heat Sauce during the last 2 minutes.

University of Flavor: The Sweet Heat Grilling Handbook

Sweet Heat BBQ Beef Brisket

Cooking Time: 6 hrs

Ingredients

- Beef brisket (3 lbs), University of Flavor Sweet Heat Sauce (1/2 cup)
- All-Purpose Seasoning (3 tbsp)
- brown sugar (2 tbsp)

Steps

1. Marinate beef cubes in Sweet Heat Sauce and All-Purpose Seasoning.
2. Skewer with onion and peppers, and grill for 4-5 mins per side.

University of Flavor: The Sweet Heat Grilling Handbook

Grilled Sweet Heat Burgers

Cooking Time: 15 mins

Ingredients

- Ground beef (1 lb), University of Flavor Sweet Heat Sauce (2 tbsp)
- All-Purpose Seasoning (2 tbsp)
- Hamburger buns
- Lettuce
- Tomato

Steps

1. Mix ground beef with Sweet Heat Sauce and All-Purpose Seasoning.
2. Form patties and grill, then assemble burgers with toppings.

University of Flavor: The Sweet Heat Grilling Handbook

Sweet Heat Glazed Meatballs

Cooking Time: 25 mins

Ingredients

- Ground beef (1 lb)
- University of Flavor Sweet Heat Sauce (1/4 cup)
- All-Purpose Seasoning (2 tbsp)
- Breadcrumbs, egg (1)

Steps

1. Mix ground beef, Sweet Heat Sauce, All-Purpose Seasoning, breadcrumbs, and egg.
2. Form meatballs and bake or grill, basting with sauce.

Sweet Heat Beef Short Ribs

Cooking Time: 2 hrs

Ingredients

- Beef short ribs (2 lbs), University of Flavor Sweet Heat Sauce (1/2 cup)
- All-Purpose Seasoning (3 tbsp)
- Beef stock (1 cup)

Steps

1. Season short ribs with All-Purpose Seasoning and grill to sear.
2. Slow-cook with beef stock and Sweet Heat Sauce until tender.

University of Flavor: The Sweet Heat Grilling Handbook

Sweet Heat Steak Tacos

Cooking Time: 20 mins (+30 mins marinating)

Ingredients

- Skirt steak (1 lb), University of Flavor Sweet Heat Sauce (1/4 cup)
- All-Purpose Seasoning (2 tbsp)
- Corn tortillas
- Cilantro
- Lime

Steps

1. Marinate steak with Sweet Heat Sauce and All-Purpose Seasoning.
2. Grill, slice, and serve on tortillas with lime and cilantro.

University of Flavor: The Sweet Heat Grilling Handbook

Sweet Heat Beef Stir-Fry

Cooking Time: 20 mins

Ingredients

- Beef strips (1 lb), University of Flavor Sweet Heat Sauce (1/4 cup)
- All-Purpose Seasoning (2 tbsp)
- Broccoli
- Bell peppers
- Soy sauce

Steps

1. Sauté beef strips with All-Purpose Seasoning.
2. Add Sweet Heat Sauce, vegetables, and soy sauce.
3. Stir-fry until tender-crisp.

University of Flavor: The Sweet Heat Grilling Handbook

Sweet Heat Stuffed Bell Peppers

Cooking Time: 45 mins

Ingredients

- Ground beef (1 lb), University of Flavor Sweet Heat Sauce (1/4 cup)
- All-Purpose Seasoning (2 tbsp)
- Bell peppers (4)
- Rice (1 cup)

Steps

1. Mix ground beef with Sweet Heat Sauce and All-Purpose Seasoning
2. Stuff peppers with beef and rice mixture, bake until tender.

University of Flavor: The Sweet Heat Grilling Handbook

Sweet Heat Chili

Cooking Time: 40 mins

Ingredients

- Ground beef (1 lb), University of Flavor Sweet Heat Sauce (1/4 cup)
- All-Purpose Seasoning (2 tbsp)
- Kidney beans
- Diced tomatoes
- Chili powder

Steps

1. Brown ground beef with All-Purpose Seasoning.
2. Add Sweet Heat Sauce, beans, tomatoes, and chili powder.
3. Simmer for 30 minutes.

Pork Recipes

University of Flavor: The Sweet Heat Grilling Handbook

Sweet Heat Grilled Pork Chops

Cooking Time: 20 mins

Ingredients

- Pork chops (4), University of Flavor Sweet Heat Sauce (1/4 cup)
- All-Purpose Seasoning (2 tbsp)
- Olive oil (2 tbsp)

Steps

1. Rub pork chops with olive oil and All-Purpose Seasoning.
2. Grill on medium heat, brushing with Sweet Heat Sauce during the last 2 minutes.

University of Flavor: The Sweet Heat Grilling Handbook

Sweet Heat Pulled Pork Sliders

Cooking Time: 6-8 hrs

Ingredients

- Pork shoulder (3 lbs)
- University of Flavor Sweet Heat Sauce (1/2 cup)
- All-Purpose Seasoning (3 tbsp)
- Apple cider vinegar (2 tbsp)

Steps

1. Rub pork shoulder with All-Purpose Seasoning.
2. Slow-cook for 6-8 hours, shredding and mixing with Sweet Heat Sauce and vinegar before serving.

University of Flavor: The Sweet Heat Grilling Handbook

Sweet Heat Glazed Pork Ribs

Cooking Time: 2.5 hrs

Ingredients

- Pork ribs (2 racks)
- University of Flavor Sweet Heat Sauce (1/2 cup)
- All-Purpose Seasoning (3 tbsp)
- Honey (2 tbsp)
- Apple cider vinegar (2 tbsp)

Steps

1. Rub ribs with All-Purpose Seasoning.
2. Grill or bake for 2 hours, then brush with Sweet Heat Sauce and cook for another 30 minutes.

University of Flavor: The Sweet Heat Grilling Handbook

Sweet Heat Pork Tenderloin

Cooking Time: 25 mins

Ingredients

- Pork tenderloin (1)
- University of Flavor Sweet Heat Sauce (1/4 cup)
- All-Purpose Seasoning (2 tbsp)
- Garlic powder (1 tsp)

Steps

1. Rub pork tenderloin with garlic powder and All-Purpose Seasoning
2. Grill on medium heat, basting with Sweet Heat Sauce until done.

University of Flavor: The Sweet Heat Grilling Handbook

Sweet Heat Pork Belly Burnt Ends

Cooking Time: 1.5 mins

Ingredients

- Pork belly (2 lbs)
- University of Flavor Sweet Heat Sauce (1/4 cup), All-Purpose Seasoning (2 tbsp)
- Honey (2 tbsp)
- Brown sugar (2 tbsp)

Steps

1. Season pork belly with All-Purpose Seasoning and roast until crispy.
2. Toss in a mixture of Sweet Heat Sauce, honey, and brown sugar.

University of Flavor: The Sweet Heat Grilling Handbook

Sweet Heat Pork Skewers

Cooking Time: 15 mins (+30 mins marinating)

Ingredients

- Pork cubes (1 lb), University of Flavor Sweet Heat Sauce (1/4 cup)
- All-Purpose Seasoning (2 tbsp)
- Pineapple chunks
- Red onion

Steps

1. Marinate pork cubes in Sweet Heat Sauce and All-Purpose Seasoning.
2. Skewer with pineapple and onion, and grill for 3-4 minutes per side.

University of Flavor: The Sweet Heat Grilling Handbook

Sweet Heat Stuffed Pork Loin

Cooking Time: 1 hr

Ingredients

- Pork loin (3 lbs)
- University of Flavor Sweet Heat Sauce (1/4 cup)
- All-Purpose Seasoning (3 tbsp)
- Spinach
- Cream cheese (1/2 cup)

Steps

1. Butterfly pork loin and fill with a mixture of spinach and cream cheese.
2. Season with All-Purpose Seasoning and bake, brushing with Sweet Heat Sauce.

University of Flavor: The Sweet Heat Grilling Handbook

Sweet Heat Pork Sausage Patties

Cooking Time: 20 mins

Ingredients

- Ground pork (1 lb)
- University of Flavor Sweet Heat Sauce (2 tbsp)
- All-Purpose Seasoning (2 tbsp)
- Breadcrumbs, egg (1)

Steps

1. Mix ground pork with Sweet Heat Sauce, All-Purpose Seasoning, breadcrumbs, and egg.
2. Form patties and grill or pan-fry until cooked through.

University of Flavor: The Sweet Heat Grilling Handbook

Sweet Heat Pork Fried Rice

Cooking Time: 15 mins

Ingredients

- Cooked pork (1 cup shredded)
- University of Flavor Sweet Heat Sauce (2 tbsp)
- All-Purpose Seasoning (2 tbsp)
- Rice (2 cups)
- Soy sauce (1 tbsp)

Steps

1. Sauté shredded pork with Sweet Heat Sauce and All-Purpose Seasoning.
2. Add to fried rice mix with soy sauce and stir until combined.

Sweet Heat BBQ Pork Meatballs

Cooking Time: 25 mins

Ingredients

- Ground pork (1 lb), University of Flavor Sweet Heat Sauce (1/4 cup)
- All-Purpose Seasoning (2 tbsp)
- Breadcrumbs
- Egg (1)

Steps

1. Mix ground pork, Sweet Heat Sauce, All-Purpose Seasoning, breadcrumbs, and egg.
2. Form meatballs and bake, basting with Sweet Heat Sauce.

Seafood Recipes

University of Flavor: The Sweet Heat Grilling Handbook

Sweet Heat Grilled Salmon

Cooking Time: 20 mins

Ingredients

- Salmon fillets (4)
- University of Flavor Sweet Heat Sauce (1/4 cup)
- All-Purpose Seasoning (2 tbsp)
- Olive oil (2 tbsp)

Steps

1. Brush salmon with olive oil and All-Purpose Seasoning.
2. Grill on medium heat, basting with Sweet Heat Sauce during the last 2 minutes.

University of Flavor: The Sweet Heat Grilling Handbook

Sweet Heat Shrimp Skewers

Cooking Time: 15 mins (+30 mins marinating)

Ingredients

- Shrimp (1 lb), University of Flavor Sweet Heat Sauce (1/4 cup)
- All-Purpose Seasoning (2 tbsp)
- Bell peppers
- Red onion

Steps

1. Marinate shrimp in Sweet Heat Sauce and All-Purpose Seasoning
2. Skewer with bell peppers and onion, and grill for 3-4 minutes per side.

University of Flavor: The Sweet Heat Grilling Handbook

Sweet Heat Glazed Tilapia

Cooking Time: 20 mins

Ingredients

- Tilapia fillets (4)
- University of Flavor Sweet Heat Sauce (1/4 cup)
- All-Purpose Seasoning (2 tbsp)
- Lime juice (1 tbsp)

Steps

1. Season tilapia with All-Purpose Seasoning and lime juice.
2. Bake or grill, basting with Sweet Heat Sauce during the last 5 minutes.

University of Flavor: The Sweet Heat Grilling Handbook

Sweet Heat Crab Cakes

Cooking Time: 25 mins

Ingredients

- Lump crab meat (1 lb)
- University of Flavor Sweet Heat Sauce (2 tbsp)
- All-Purpose Seasoning (2 tbsp)
- Breadcrumbs, egg (1)

Steps

1. Mix crab meat, Sweet Heat Sauce, All-Purpose Seasoning, breadcrumbs, and egg.
2. Form into cakes and pan-fry until golden.

University of Flavor: The Sweet Heat Grilling Handbook

Sweet Heat Lobster Tails

Cooking Time: 15 mins

Ingredients

- Lobster tails (4), University of Flavor Sweet Heat Sauce (1/4 cup)
- All-Purpose Seasoning (2 tbsp)
- Melted butter (2 tbsp)

Steps

1. Brush lobster tails with melted butter and Sweet Heat Sauce
2. Sprinkle with All-Purpose Seasoning and grill for 5-7 minutes.

University of Flavor: The Sweet Heat Grilling Handbook

Sweet Heat Scallops

Cooking Time: 15 mins

Ingredients

- Scallops (1 lb)
- University of Flavor Sweet Heat Sauce (1/4 cup)
- All-Purpose Seasoning (2 tbsp)
- Olive oil (2 tbsp)

Steps

1. Pat scallops dry and season with All-Purpose Seasoning.
2. Sear in a hot pan with olive oil, basting with Sweet Heat Sauce.

University of Flavor: The Sweet Heat Grilling Handbook

Sweet Heat Shrimp Tacos

Cooking Time: 20 mins

Ingredients

- Shrimp (1 lb)
- University of Flavor Sweet Heat Sauce (1/4 cup)
- All-Purpose Seasoning (2 tbsp)
- Corn tortillas
- Cabbage slaw

Steps

1. Cook shrimp with All-Purpose Seasoning.
2. Assemble tacos with shrimp, cabbage slaw, and Sweet Heat Sauce drizzle.

University of Flavor: The Sweet Heat Grilling Handbook

Sweet Heat Grilled Mahi-Mahi

Cooking Time: 20 mins

Ingredients

- Mahi-Mahi fillets (4)
- University of Flavor Sweet Heat Sauce (1/4 cup)
- All-Purpose Seasoning (2 tbsp)
- Lime juice (1 tbsp)

Steps

1. Rub Mahi-Mahi fillets with All-Purpose Seasoning.
2. Grill on medium heat, basting with Sweet Heat Sauce and lime juice.

University of Flavor: The Sweet Heat Grilling Handbook

Sweet Heat Seafood Paella

Cooking Time: 40 mins

Ingredients

- Mixed seafood (shrimp, mussels, clams, 2 lbs)
- University of Flavor Sweet Heat Sauce (1/4 cup)
- All-Purpose Seasoning (3 tbsp)
- Rice
- Chicken stock

Steps

1. Sauté mixed seafood with All-Purpose Seasoning.
2. Add rice, chicken stock, and Sweet Heat Sauce, simmering until rice is cooked.

University of Flavor: The Sweet Heat Grilling Handbook

Sweet Heat Baked Cod

Cooking Time: 25 mins

Ingredients

- Cod fillets (4)
- University of Flavor Sweet Heat Sauce (1/4 cup)
- All-Purpose Seasoning (2 tbsp)
- Breadcrumbs
- Parmesan cheese (2 tbsp)

Steps

1. Brush cod with Sweet Heat Sauce and coat with breadcrumbs and Parmesan.
2. Bake until golden and flaky.

Grilled Chicken Recipes

University of Flavor: The Sweet Heat Grilling Handbook

Sweet Heat Grilled Chicken Thighs

Cooking Time: 30 mins (+2 hrs marinating)

Ingredients

- Bone-in chicken thighs
- University of Flavor Sweet Heat Sauce (1/4 cup)
- All-Purpose Seasoning (3 tbsp)
- Olive oil (2 tbsp)
- Apple cider vinegar (2 tbsp)

Steps

1. Rub chicken with oil and coat with All-Purpose Seasoning.
2. Grill on medium heat, basting with Sweet Heat Sauce and vinegar mix.

University of Flavor: The Sweet Heat Grilling Handbook

Honey Lime Glazed Chicken Breasts

Cooking Time: 25 mins (+2 hrs marinating)

Ingredients

- Chicken breasts (4)
- University of Flavor Sweet Heat Sauce (2 tbsp)
- Honey (2 tbsp)
- Lime juice (2 tbsp)
- All-Purpose Seasoning (2 tbsp)
- Garlic (2 cloves minced)

Steps

1. Combine Sweet Heat Sauce, honey, lime juice, and All-Purpose Seasoning.
2. Marinate chicken for 2 hours. Grill on medium-high, basting with marinade.

University of Flavor: The Sweet Heat Grilling Handbook

Spicy Grilled Buffalo Drumsticks

Cooking Time: 25 mins

Ingredients

- Chicken drumsticks (8)
- University of Flavor Sweet Heat Sauce (1/4 cup)
- All-Purpose Seasoning (2 tbsp)
- Melted butter (2 tbsp)

Steps

1. Season drumsticks with All-Purpose Seasoning.
2. Grill for 20-25 mins, tossing in Sweet Heat Sauce mixed with butter before serving.

University of Flavor: The Sweet Heat Grilling Handbook

Mango-Chipotle Chicken Wings

Cooking Time: 20 mins

Ingredients

- Chicken wings (2 lbs)
- University of Flavor Sweet Heat Sauce (1/4 cup)
- All-Purpose Seasoning (2 tbsp)
- Mango puree (1/2 cup)

Steps

1. Blend Sweet Heat Sauce, mango puree, and All-Purpose Seasoning for glaze.
2. Grill wings, coat with glaze, and cook an additional 3 mins per side.

University of Flavor: The Sweet Heat Grilling Handbook

Lemon Herb Spatchcock Chicken

Cooking Time: 45 mins

Ingredients

- Whole chicken (spatchcocked, 1)
- University of Flavor Sweet Heat Sauce (3 tbsp)
- All-Purpose Seasoning (2 tbsp)
- Olive oil (3 tbsp)
- Lemon zest (2 tbsp)

Steps

1. Rub chicken with olive oil, All-Purpose Seasoning, and lemon zest.
2. Grill over indirect heat for 30-40 mins, basting with Sweet Heat Sauce during the last 10 mins.

University of Flavor: The Sweet Heat Grilling Handbook

Sweet Heat Chicken Skewers

Cooking Time: 45 mins

Ingredients

- Chicken thighs (cubed, 1 lb)
- University of Flavor Sweet Heat Sauce (2 tbsp)
- All-Purpose Seasoning (2 tbsp)
- Pineapple chunks (1 cup)
- Bell peppers (1 cup)

Steps

1. Toss chicken in Sweet Heat Sauce and All-Purpose Seasoning.
2. Skewer with pineapple and peppers. Grill on medium for 3-4 mins per side.

University of Flavor: The Sweet Heat Grilling Handbook

BBQ Bacon-Wrapped Chicken Tenders

Cooking Time: 20 mins

Ingredients

- Chicken tenders (1 lb)
- University of Flavor Sweet Heat Sauce (1/4 cup)
- All-Purpose Seasoning (2 tbsp)
- Bacon (12 slices)

Steps

1. Season tenders with All-Purpose Seasoning. Wrap each tender in bacon.
2. Grill on medium, brushing with Sweet Heat Sauce until crispy.

Coconut Curry Grilled Chicken Thighs

Cooking Time: 25 mins (+4 hrs marinating)

Ingredients

- Chicken thighs (1 lb)
- University of Flavor Sweet Heat Sauce (2 tbsp)
- All-Purpose Seasoning (2 tbsp)
- Coconut milk (1 cup)
- Curry powder (2 tsp)

Steps

1. Marinate chicken in coconut milk, curry powder, Sweet Heat Sauce, and All-Purpose Seasoning for 4 hours.
2. Grill until charred and fully cooked.

University of Flavor: The Sweet Heat Grilling Handbook

Sweet Heat BBQ Pulled Chicken Sandwiches

Cooking Time: 30 mins

Ingredients

- Chicken breasts (4)
- University of Flavor Sweet Heat Sauce (1/4 cup)
- All-Purpose Seasoning (2 tbsp)
- Barbecue sauce (1/2 cup)
- Apple cider vinegar (1 tbsp)

Steps

1. Season chicken with All-Purpose Seasoning and grill until done.
2. Shred and mix with Sweet Heat Sauce and barbecue sauce. Serve on toasted buns with slaw.

University of Flavor: The Sweet Heat Grilling Handbook

Peach Bourbon Glazed Chicken Halves

Cooking Time: 45 mins

Ingredients

- Chicken halves (2)
- University of Flavor Sweet Heat Sauce (1/4 cup)
- All-Purpose Seasoning (3 tbsp)
- Peach preserves (1/3 cup)
- Bourbon (2 tbsp)

Steps

1. Mix Sweet Heat Sauce, peach preserves, bourbon, and All-Purpose Seasoning for glaze.
2. Grill chicken halves 30-40 mins over indirect heat, basting with glaze.

Vegetable Recipes

University of Flavor: The Sweet Heat Grilling Handbook

Sweet Heat Grilled Vegetable Medley

Cooking Time: 15-20 mins

Ingredients

- Zucchini
- Bell peppers
- Red onion
- University of Flavor Sweet Heat Sauce (1/4 cup)
- All-Purpose Seasoning (2 tbsp)
- Olive oil (2 tbsp)

Steps

1. Toss vegetables in olive oil, All-Purpose Seasoning, and Sweet Heat Sauce.
2. Grill on medium heat until tender and charred.

University of Flavor: The Sweet Heat Grilling Handbook

Sweet Heat Roasted Brussels Sprouts

Cooking Time: 20-25 mins

Ingredients

- Brussels sprouts (1 lb)
- University of Flavor Sweet Heat Sauce (1/4 cup)
- All-Purpose Seasoning (2 tbsp)
- Olive oil (2 tbsp)

Steps

1. Toss Brussels sprouts in olive oil, All-Purpose Seasoning, and Sweet Heat Sauce.
2. Roast at 400Â°F for 20-25 minutes.

University of Flavor: The Sweet Heat Grilling Handbook

Sweet Heat Glazed Carrots

Cooking Time: 25-30 mins

Ingredients

- Carrots (1 lb)
- University of Flavor Sweet Heat Sauce (1/4 cup)
- All-Purpose Seasoning (2 tbsp)
- Honey (1 tbsp)

Steps

1. Glaze carrots with Sweet Heat Sauce, All-Purpose Seasoning, and honey.
2. Roast at 400°F for 25-30 minutes until caramelized.

University of Flavor: The Sweet Heat Grilling Handbook

Sweet Heat Stuffed Bell Peppers

Cooking Time: 25-30 mins

Ingredients

- Bell peppers (4)
- Cooked rice (1 cup)
- University of Flavor Sweet Heat Sauce (2 tbsp)
- All-Purpose Seasoning (2 tbsp)
- Black beans (1/2 cup)

Steps

1. Mix rice, beans, Sweet Heat Sauce, and All-Purpose Seasoning.
2. Stuff bell peppers and bake at 375°F for 25-30 minutes.

University of Flavor: The Sweet Heat Grilling Handbook

Sweet Heat Spiced Cauliflower Steaks

Cooking Time: 20-25 mins

Ingredients

- Cauliflower steaks (4 slices)
- University of Flavor Sweet Heat Sauce (1/4 cup)
- All-Purpose Seasoning (2 tbsp)
- Olive oil (2 tbsp)

Steps

1. Brush cauliflower steaks with olive oil, All-Purpose Seasoning, and Sweet Heat Sauce.
2. Roast or grill until tender and browned.

University of Flavor: The Sweet Heat Grilling Handbook

Sweet Heat Roasted Sweet Potatoes

Cooking Time: 25-30 mins

Ingredients

- Sweet potatoes (2 large)
- University of Flavor Sweet Heat Sauce (1/4 cup)
- All-Purpose Seasoning (2 tbsp)
- Brown sugar (1 tbsp)

Steps

1. Coat sweet potato slices with All-Purpose Seasoning, Sweet Heat Sauce, and brown sugar.
2. Roast at 400°F for 25-30 minutes.

Sweet Heat Grilled Portobello Mushrooms

Cooking Time: 10-12 mins

Ingredients

- Portobello mushrooms (4)
- University of Flavor Sweet Heat Sauce (1/4 cup)
- All-Purpose Seasoning (2 tbsp)
- Balsamic vinegar (1 tbsp)

Steps

1. Marinate mushrooms in Sweet Heat Sauce, All-Purpose Seasoning, and balsamic vinegar.
2. Grill for 4-5 minutes per side.

Sweet Heat Sautéed Green Beans

Cooking Time: 20-25 mins

Ingredients

- Green beans (1 lb)
- University of Flavor Sweet Heat Sauce (2 tbsp)
- All-Purpose Seasoning (2 tbsp)
- Garlic (2 cloves minced)

Steps

1. Sauté green beans in olive oil with garlic. Toss in Sweet Heat Sauce and All-Purpose Seasoning.
2. Cook until tender-crisp.

University of Flavor: The Sweet Heat Grilling Handbook

Sweet Heat Baked Zucchini Fries

Cooking Time: 20-25 mins

Ingredients

- Zucchini (2 large)
- Breadcrumbs
- University of Flavor Sweet Heat Sauce (2 tbsp)
- All-Purpose Seasoning (2 tbsp)
- Parmesan cheese (2 tbsp)

Steps

1. Dip zucchini slices in Sweet Heat Sauce, coat with breadcrumbs mixed with All-Purpose Seasoning and Parmesan.
2. Bake at 425Â°F until crispy.

University of Flavor: The Sweet Heat Grilling Handbook

Sweet Heat BBQ Veggie Skewers

Cooking Time: 15-20 mins

Ingredients

- Zucchini
- Cherry tomatoes
- Mushrooms
- University of Flavor Sweet Heat Sauce (1/4 cup)
- All-Purpose Seasoning (2 tbsp)

Steps

1. Marinate veggies in Sweet Heat Sauce and All-Purpose Seasoning.
2. Skewer and grill for 4-5 minutes per side.

About the Author:

Troy Washington is a passionate culinary artist, entrepreneur, and the visionary behind University of Flavor. Known for his signature approach to bold, balanced flavors, Troy has dedicated his career to creating unforgettable taste experiences. Starting with his beloved sauce company, he turned his love for grilling and seasonings into a movement, blending tradition with innovation.

With a focus on "sweet heat" and all-purpose versatility, Troy's cooking philosophy is simple: great food brings people together. His grilling cookbook is not just a guide—it's an invitation to explore, experiment, and celebrate the art of barbecue.

When he's not perfecting recipes, Troy spends time inspiring others to master their craft and embrace the magic of flavors in everyday cooking.

Made in the USA
Columbia, SC
11 January 2025